Wonders of Swamps and Marshes

Written by Stephen Caitlin

Illustrated by James Watling

Troll Associates

Library of Congress Cataloging-in-Publication Data

Caitlin, Stephen.
 Wonders of swamps and marshes / by Stephen Caitlin; illustrated
by James Watling.
   p.   cm.
   Summary: Describes swamps and marshes and the ecological systems
which they support.
   ISBN 0-8167-1765-6 (lib. bdg.)   ISBN 0-8167-1766-4 (pbk.)
   1. Swamp ecology—Juvenile literature.   2. Swamps—Juvenile
literature.   3. Marsh ecology—Juvenile literature.   4. Marshes—
Juvenile literature.   [1. Swamp ecology.   2. Marsh ecology.
3. Ecology.]   I. Watling, James, ill.   II. Title.
QH541.5.S9C35   1990
574.5´26325—dc20   89-4967

It is a warm, summer night. Beneath the rising moon, the swamp comes alive. Listen carefully to the sounds of this special world.

Splash! A fish jumps in a nearby stream. An owl hoots its lonely call. *Jug-o-rum!* A bullfrog adds its croaking song. Among the twigs and grass, a mouse scurries by. It hopes to escape a hungry snake.

Swamps and marshes are the watery homes of countless plants and animals. Let's explore these strange, yet beautiful lands. They are filled with many surprises.

What makes a swamp or marsh? The most important ingredient is water. Marshes and swamps are lowlands that are soaked by water. Just as its name says, a *lowland* is a low piece of land. Water collects there and cannot drain away because the area is lower than the land around it. Another name for such a place is a *wetland*.

Marshes and swamps are two kinds of wetlands. The biggest difference between a swamp and a marsh is the kind of plants that grows in each.

In a swamp, trees, bushes, and shrubs grow. A marsh is
different. It has no trees or woody plants. Instead, marshes are
filled with many kinds of grass and grasslike plants. Tall cattails, slender reeds, and rough-edged saw grass are just a few of
the plants that may grow in a marsh.

There are swamps and marshes throughout the world.
Some marshes form in the open, wide lowlands of the prairie.
The lands near rivers and along seacoasts also make up
wetlands.

Do you think a marsh can be found in the desert? Or could a marsh form in the frozen land of the far North?

Surprisingly, the answer to both questions is "yes." If there is a spring of water nearby, a desert marsh may form. And in the frozen earth of the North, there is a place called the *tundra*. This land thaws, or melts, for a short time in summer. The tundra becomes a marsh, dotted with beautiful wildflowers. Many birds, insects, and other animals raise their young in the tundra during the short summer season.

All swamps and marshes are watery, but do you know what kind of water they have in them? Some have fresh water. Others are made by a combination of fresh and salt water. This happens along the coasts, where the ocean's salty water meets freshwater rivers and ponds. Where these waters meet, a *salt marsh* is created.

The salt marsh is rich in life. Red-winged blackbirds dart through the air, searching for insects to feed their babies. These pretty birds make their nests among the tall cattails. Many other birds also live in the salt marsh—the large osprey and the delicate-looking sandpiper are two of them.

In fall, the salt marsh is a sheltered place, full of food. Thousands of ducks and geese, flying to warm southern lands for the winter, stop off at the marsh to eat and rest.

By night, raccoons search for fish and berries to eat. And out of sight, buried in the wet sand, live other creatures. Two such underground animals are the soft-shell clam and the burrowing starfish.

11

During high tide, the moon's pull on the ocean causes the salty sea water to flood the marsh. The sandy homes of the clam and starfish are flooded with water rich in minerals and other tiny bits of food. The starfish and clam suck the nourishing water down through small holes in the sand. If you should visit a salt marsh, look closely in the sand for these tiny holes—they are the "doors" to the secret, underground homes of these unusual animals.

At low tide, the salty ocean water drains from the marsh and goes back out to sea. The everyday flooding and emptying of water is very important, both to life in the marsh and to life in the ocean.

By bringing nourishing salt water, flooding creates a rich growing place for the plants and animals of the marsh. And when the salt water drains away at low tide, it carries bits of dead plants and animals from the marsh. These materials are taken far out to sea, where they become food for fish that live in deep waters.

One of these fish may someday find its way to your very own dinner table. So, in a way, life in the salt marsh helps to furnish food for people, too!

Different kinds of plants grow in the many different swamps of the world. Along certain warm seacoasts, there is a special kind of wetland called a *mangrove swamp*. It is named for the mangrove tree, which lives there.

The mangrove tree stands above the water on roots that look like stilts. These tangled roots hold the tree's trunk up above the water. Many creatures live in the shelter given by the roots. Small fish dart among the roots, where larger fish or animals cannot reach them. And in the mangrove's branches, big brown pelicans make their nests.

Perhaps the most interesting thing about mangrove trees is that they help to build land. Here's how: When dead plants and mud collect among the mangrove's twisting roots, soil is built up. Bit by bit, an island is created. It may become the home of animals and other plants.

Scientists have a special name for the communities of plants and animals that live together in a particular place. They call such a community an *ecosystem*.

The ecosystem of a woodland swamp is fascinating to watch. This kind of wetland is a forest that is flooded by a freshwater pond or stream. The water there usually is not very deep.

Look carefully among the trees and bushes. The nests of many insects and birds are hidden there. A mother deer and her white-spotted fawn make their way through the tangled vines and muddy land, searching for tasty berries. The baby's spots help this animal to blend in among the shadows and sunbeams of the swamp.

Turtles, fish, minks, mosquitoes, rabbits, foxes, bears, and many other creatures live in the swamp. Each is able to survive, or stay alive, because it can find food to eat. But in the ecosystem of the swamp, this means that an animal living there may one day become food for another animal.

Here is what happens: Sun, water, and soil nourish many growing plants. In turn, some of the plants may become food for a small mouse. The mouse may be caught and eaten by a fox. And, in turn, the fox may be caught by a wildcat. Unused food leaves the wildcat's body as waste. Little by little, this waste matter breaks down into rich soil. In the rich soil, more plants will grow—and the circle will begin again.

This furnishing of food for one another is called a *food chain*. Each plant or animal in an ecosystem makes up a link in the chain. The food chain is nature's way of keeping a balance between all the living things in an ecosystem.

Each wetland ecosystem has its own combination of plants and animals. There are several famous wetlands. One is in Florida, and it is called the *Everglades*. This freshwater marsh is the largest in the world. It is also called the "river of grass," a name that describes this marsh very well. In fact, there is so much water beneath the wide prairies of tall, waving grass, that special boats, called airboats, are used to travel through the Everglades.

A large lake floods this special marsh. Fish and other water animals live in its shallow waters. These creatures often become food for the brightly colored birds that live in the Everglades.

Pelicans fly low over the water, scooping up fish in their big beaks. But many of the birds that hunt for fish must be careful that they do not become the meal of a hungry alligator.

Another unique wetland is found in Georgia. This southern swamp is called the *Okefenokee.* This is an Indian word that means "trembling earth." The name is a good one, for in some spots, the earth does shake. This is because the earth is so watery that the roots of many plants are not tightly anchored, or attached, to the land.

Two rivers begin in the Okefenokee, creating this fresh-water swamp. In spring, beautiful orchid flowers bloom. Insects buzz everywhere. The giant cypress trees of the swamp make a beautiful sight. Their branches are draped by long pieces of Spanish moss, a lovely, lacy-looking plant.

The animal life of the Okefenokee swamp is also very rich. Rattlesnakes, turtles, black bears, and bobcats are just a few of the creatures that live there.

Alligators swim through the water of the swamp. The grown alligators build nests made of plants. Then they lay their eggs. As soon as they hatch, off the baby alligators head for the water.

All swamps and marshes are exciting places to explore. These wetlands are not just important to the animals and plants that live there. They are also very important to people. These special lands give us their beauty. And they offer us the rare chance to watch the world of nature at work. By studying these wetlands, we can see how they form an important link in the world's food chain.

In addition, swamps and marshes serve as a storage place for one of our most precious resources—water. By storing great amounts of water, they help to reduce floods and erosion, the wearing away of the earth by water.

These strangely beautiful lands, with their special plants and animals, are fascinating to observe. They are one of nature's most unique creations.